The Talk I Never Had for girls
by Jordan C. and Shermane Reed

Amazon Kindle Direct Publishing
2019

Copyright – October 2019

ISBN – 13 ISBN # 978-0-578-59034-9

The Talk I Never Had for girls
Jordan C. Reed and Shermane Reed

Illustrated by Therese Seghers

Edited by Nedra Epps
Vision Heirs Publishing and Consulting

Scripture references: New International Version Copyright © 1973, 1978, 1984, 2011 by Biblica; New Living Translation Copyright © 1996, 2004, 2015 by Tyndale House; New American Standard Bible Copyright © 1960, 1962, 1963, 1968, 1971, 1972, 1973, 1975, 1977, 1995 by The Lockman Foundation

Stay Tuned For JC the Slayer a Comic Series
Devotional for girls
and Beautifully Broken: A Survivor Speaks and
Transforms a bible study for women

This book belongs to:

____

Was given by:

____

Because:

____

The Talk I Never Had
for girls

The Talk I Never Had is a look into the life of a pre-teen girl named Jordan. Within this book Jordan shares her diary and thoughts as her body begins a metamorphosis right before her eyes. She is not afraid to ask God those hard, confusing questions about His creation and her body. Jordan shares relatable, encouraging and empowering stories of embracing your body as the valuable treasure it is. She will inspire each girl to write her own hygiene plan, create a HelloFlo calendar and develop a life verse. Through conversations with her mom, Jordan learns the proper anatomical names of her body parts, the stages of puberty to adulthood and, most of all, that the Creator of all things created her and her body for a divine purpose. Jordan embraces the truth that she is fearfully and wonderfully made.

Jordan and Shermane

Included with this book is a bookmark with Jordan's life verse!

Charm is deceptive, and beauty is fleeting; but a woman who fears the Lord is to be praised. (Proverbs 31:30)

Jordan Reed and her mother, Shermane Reed, reside in Lafayette, Louisiana. Jordan is a God-fearing young lady with a compassionate heart. Jordan attends a Lafayette Parish school where she loves to play piano, read, write and draw. Outside of school, Jordan loves gymnastics and cooking. Also, Jordan is a student at CYT (Christian Youth Theatre) in Lafayette, Louisiana.

Shermane is a wife, mother, inspirational speaker, and the founder of Determined To Rise Ministry - a nonprofit ministry that empowers female abuse survivors to restart, reclaim, and restore their lives in safe, Christ-centered environments. *The Talk I Never Had* is meant to encourage young girls (ages 8-13) and mothers to have "the talk." Shermane strongly believes it is important for every daughter to know their mother's story. This is truly *The Talk I Never Had*. It is our goal to go into communities, schools, and churches and have "the talk" with other moms and daughters.

Dedication

For all the girls in the world
who need the talk or missed the talk;
this book is dedicated to you. For all the girls in the world
whose mom may not be here; this book is for you.

Embrace The Change

Thanks to my mom. Though she never had the talk, she
has given me the most encouraging talk about my body and
loving myself that I could ever imagine. You are the best,
Mom. I love you to the red slushie and back. Thanks to my
dad who has taught me what love is and showered me with
love. I could not dream of a better family than my own.

Thanks to my school, J Wallace James Arts Academy.
Thanks to my fourth-grade teacher,
Mrs. Erin Cuccio, for encouraging us to write essays,
paragraphs, letters and the many narrative stories that have
helped me write this book.

Love, Jordan

To Jordan Chavise Reed,
my dearest daughter

Writing this book with you was an absolute pleasure. You are an amazing young lady. I am so proud of you. I know you want to be just like me, but you will be better than me. Great! You will be a wonderful woman of God, wife, and mother. I pray I get to see all the things that God will do in and through your life. I have already prayed over your husband and my grandchildren that are far from now. You are a rare and valuable treasure. I pray you never neglect your first marriage which is to God.

Table of Contents

To All Girls

Dear Girls,

My name is Jordan. I am so excited that you are reading my book. Did you know there will never be a shortage of girls in the world? There are TONS of girls in the world! That means there are tons of moms in the world! I am blessed with a pretty amazing mom. I hope that you are too.

However, my biggest fear is losing my mom. So, I do know that there are some girls in the world who have lost their moms. I want you to know I cannot relate to that deep loss you may feel, but I can lend you my mom. As you read through this book, when you see my mom speaking, listen for the voice of your mom through my mom. If you have never heard the voice of your mom, listen to my mom's voice. She's cool. She wrote a poem dedicated to all the girls in the world who have lost their moms.

Soar Away

This is the day,
I am most afraid.
My mom left me,
And never returned home.

I became a lost girl,
Right there.
I jumped in a spacesuit,
And floated off to nowhere.

The moment
I shut my eyes,
I saw God
Soaring high.

Jesus found me.
He had the brightest smile.
Asked if He could talk to me,
His child

He said,
Yahweh that's the name they call
Him,
I want to tell you, through Me
You will be family.

And after that very day,

No more a lost girl
from nowhere,
Leaving now with Jesus
Finally soaring somewhere.

Together we flew,
as we passed Mars.
He reached out
And gave me a star. He said
Shine, Shine, Bright Girl
Soar Away.

Shine, Shine, Bright Girl

Soar Away.

Jesus Christ is home
for girls like me;
And in He
we have family!

CREATION

"In the beginning God created the heavens and the Earth. Now the earth was formless, and empty, darkness was on the face of the deep, and the Spirit of God was hovering over of the waters. And God said, "Let there be light," and there was light." Genesis 1:1-3

Can you believe He created the world in 5 days? And on day 6, after God had created all the creatures that live on dry land, God said, "Let us make man in our own image, after our likeness:" Genesis 1:26

God is the creator of all things. The earth is the Lord's, and everything in it, the world, and all who live in it. Psalm 24:1

Chapter One

Why am I Special?

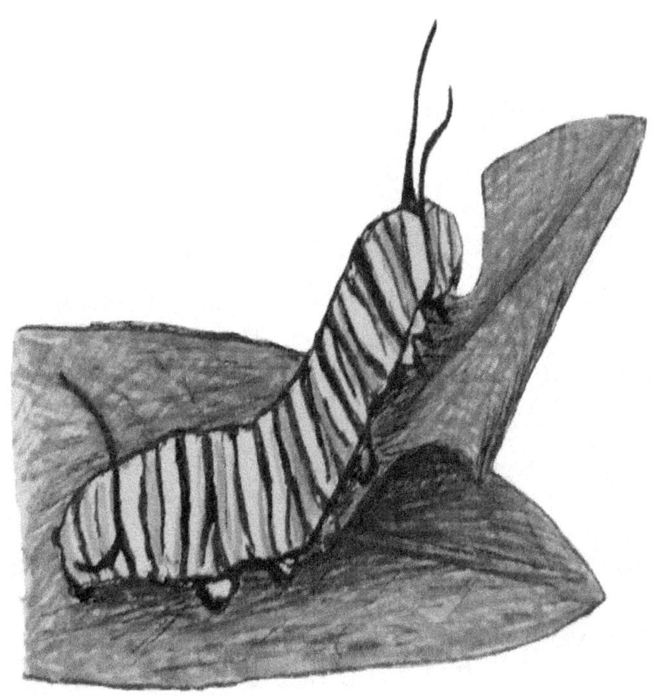

Dear Diary,

It's Jordan and I have a really big question for God. God created humans in his image. So, does that mean we look like God? Does that make me special? Does that mean God is part woman? I am soooo confused right now.

Dear Jordan,

God loves you so much. You are unique, one of a kind, unlike anything else. When God created man, He created them, male and female. Can you imagine God right now creating you? He created everything, Did you know that after He created man, He had a special thought?

God said, "It is not good for man to be alone. I will make him a helper who is like him."

The man found no suitable helper. Did you know that God thought you were so special, He caused man to go into a deep sleep just to create you? As man slept, God uniquely and masterfully created you. Yes, you. Just you and God. How special is that? God took out special, one on one time just to create you. He took one of man's rib and closed his flesh as man slept. Then, the Lord God made the rib He had taken from man into a woman. You are very special my child. God uniquely orchestrated you. He took out special time to create a special woman! Never forget how special you are.

Love, Mom

... ₒₒOO

"Well, mom, if I am so special, then why am I going through all of this. I hate my glasses; they are calling me a nerd. I have braces and glasses. I am dying here."

"Jordan, a nerd is a good word and braces ... hey ... that means you will have beautiful teeth. It is not that bad."

"On my scale one to ten, this is a ten hundred? I am not going to school. Homeschool me, please!"

"I wish life was that easy, but it is not. There are situations in life you have to just go through, my love."

"But why me, mom."

"You will be fine, Jordan. Going through stuff ..."

"Yeah. yeah. Makes you stronger ... I know mom."

Dear Diary,

Thank you for summertime, finally! Time to get my swim on. Um ... I still have these hairy legs. Maybe my mom will let me shave them now. I am nine; she should. I passed the third grade, so I should get a graduating gift - shaved legs. Fourth grade here I come.

... ₒₒOO

"Mom, so I've been thinking. I know you're going to say no to this question; but can I please, please, please shave my legs?"

"Nope. Maybe when you're in 6th grade, Jordan. I just don't see what the big rush is to shave your legs."

"But they are hairy. I'm looking like Chewbacca over here."

"Really, Jordan?"

"By the time I'm in sixth grade I'll be able to braid my hair on my legs!"

"It's not happening Jordan."

"Why am I so hairy? My friend's moms let them shave. Mom, I have hair everywhere, like everywhere, even down there!"

"Jordan, we have already talked about this. I understand you're self-conscious and embarrassed about your hair growth. But I want you to remember that this is the process of becoming a young lady, and it is natural and normal. When the time comes for you to shave, I promise I will personally teach you how to safely shave your legs."

"Okay. Well until then I will wear pants only."

"Hey! Look at the bright side of this. Shaving is an unnecessary habit. You are a kid. Why waste your brief childhood maintaining a habit when you don't have to? You will be an adult much longer than you'll ever be a kid. Now go get me some lotion, so I can help lay down that hair on your beautiful brown legs."

For some reason my mom always knows what to say to make me feel better about myself. "Here's the lotion mom."

Chapter Two

Buds are Buddies

Dear Diary,

It is Jordan. I am very embarrassed about my body. My chest has been hurting for about a week now. I think I am getting those things my mom calls breast.

My mom said her mom never talked to her about puberty. All the girls at school are talking about puberty. Lately, I have been thinking about what puberty means.

What does puberty mean? Yes, I googled it. I was thinking puberty is when you are becoming more mature, like you get taller and grow hair. However, when I googled it, it said puberty is when your body goes through physical changes - when a child's body matures into an adult body. It also said girls start puberty around the ages of ten to eleven and ends around seventeen. That is my entire life!

Ok, back to the buds because, as I am lying here writing, my chest is hurting. I wonder if I will have to wear a bra. All the other girls at school were talking about bras. Am I going to have to wear a bra? I hope it is just a sports bra and not one of those big bras with pads, you know.

My mom told me when you get your breast buds, if you wear a plain shirt people can see your nipples. I hope she doesn't make me watch anymore videos. They were very uncomfortable. I will have to write later; my chest is really hurting. I think I am going to tell my mom. This is not fun anymore!!

... ₒₒOO

"Mom, can you come here please? Just you, no one else."

"What is going on? Why are you crying? What happened?"

"I have a knot in my chest, and it really hurts."

"Awe, can I take a look?"

"No. I don't want you to see. It is really embarrassing. But it really hurts."

"I understand. Momma went through the same stuff when I was your age. I was really scared. I know you feel embarrassed about it, but there is nothing to be ashamed of. Your body, every part of it, has a purpose."

"Ok. You can look."

"So, my dear, this is perfectly normal. You are going through puberty! This knot underneath your nipple is a breast "bud." Let me check the other side. Eventually, the other side will have a bud as well. I noticed while I was checking your breast that you have more hair underneath your arm. Let me see your underarm. So, sometimes with increased body hair comes what you are experiencing - increased sweating and body odor. How about you and I take some time to create a body hygiene plan? I will make you a pre puberty doctor's appointment just to make sure your buds are buds."

"That is not funny mom. Ok. But don't tell anyone ... Pinky Swear"

"I promise."

Jordan's Body Facts: Everyone grows breast "buds" at different times. It will be sore, and you may feel itchy around your nipple. But remember, this is perfectly normal. What do buds grow into? Some have buds. Some have blossoms.

Jordan's Jokes: Knock, knock. Who's there? Bud. Bud who? The bud next to you.

Dear Diary,

Today is filled with stuff to do. My mom is a stay at home mom. She is like a machine; she never stops. She has stuff planned like crazy every day. I told her, when I am a mom, I hope I am just like her. She told me I will be better than her. So, today I am sharing with you the importance of my hygiene plan. I will admit my mom is right; I do need one. It is not as hard as I thought it would have been. I have to remember to look at it every morning until I have the routine down. I will share a visual of my hygiene plan below. I used a piece of paper and got creative with my plan. I added pictures - some with words and some without - so I just know the meaning. I hung the paper with tape on my dresser mirror, because looking at myself every day is important, and I will see the plan. It doesn't take much to make a simple hygiene plan. Use my example to help you make your personal hygiene plan. It can be as simple as a checklist or a picture board.

☑ Rise and Shine You are Loved!
☐ Use bathroom (pee, wash face, brush teeth)
☐ Underarm check (I sweat at night, so I make sure to check to see if more deodorant is needed from that night. I put on deodorant at night after I bathe because I was forgetting to put some on in the morning. If I am sweaty I have two options. I can take a quick shower or get a soapy towel and clean my underarms, then apply deodorant. NEVER put deodorant on top of musk. It only makes it stink worse.)
☐ Do hair, put on clean clothes, lotion
☐ Pray and eat breakfast
☐ School, be active, drink water
☐ Bath and eat dinner
☐ Brush teeth, floss

Sleep and Repeat!

Jordan's Hygiene Plan

☆ Rise and Shine
You are Valuable!

1. Wake up!

2. Make bed

You are beautiful

5. Pray

6. EAT

H₂O

7. School
be active

8. Home
Bath or Shower

9. Eat dinner

10. Floss

11. PRAY

12. Sleep zᶻᶻ and Repeat!

Chapter Three

Attack of the Pimples

Dear Diary,

I know I have been writing in you a lot, but I am going through a catastrophe here. The pimples are eating me alive! As they erupt, they look like Mount Vesuvius. Every time I walk into class people stare at me. My teachers even stare at me sometimes. #EMBARRASSING

As I walked into the lunchroom, a boy held up a huge slice of pizza and said, "Hey, look pepperoni face is here." I was so embarrassed. The rest of the day people stared at me. I got so mad I wanted to punch that boy in the face; but I didn't. I went to the restroom and tried my best to pop them, but that only made it worse. One pimple started to bleed.

I am so self-conscious and ugly. These pimples are making a home on my chin and all their grandkids and parents are moving on in.

Yes, God says I am beautiful, but I have prayed that He will make my face look beautiful. And guess what? That wish has not come true. Who made pimples anyway? (God, you made them, too!) Old people have pimples. Oh, wait. Those are moles. Do I have moles? Hold on.

Okay, I'm back. I ran to the bathroom to check to see if I had a mole. I looked in the mirror and there was a black dot. I said out loud I'm becoming a witch. Bad thing was my mom barged in.

... ooOO

"What did you just say, Jordan?"

"I am sure you misunderstood me. I said "witch."

"What do you mean 'witch'?"

"You know those old women with bumpy faces and wrinkly arms; that is me right now."

"Okay. So, what are you saying to yourself?"

"It's none of your business, mom!"

"Excuse me?"

"I have glasses, I have braces, my entire body is covered in hair like a wolf, and now I have pimples! You happy now? PUBERTY."

Dear Diary,

I just walked away from my mom and slammed my door. My mom is getting on my last nerve, asking me all these questions. I don't want to talk to anyone. She will be at my door in a minute. There she is. She did not even KNOCK! Why can't she just leave me alone? Go away! Privacy. Let's see if she understands.

My mom is like a long boring episode of Bunk'd right now. Here she goes. "Jordan,

I do not know what has gotten into you; but your behavior is not acceptable. First, you are not to slam a door in this house. Secondly, you will watch your tone with me, or you will be on punishment. Now, let's stop and pray about everything that has been going on, and we can talk about it and your feelings."

FEELINGS! FEELINGS! How are you feeling? Can you believe she sat with me and made me make a feelings chart with her, so we are able to better communicate? My mom is from another planet. I am sure of this.

The Way I Feel?

Feeling Chart

ATTACK of the PIMPLES
Where is your outbreak?

1. Simply put ... "hello 'puberty'." Don't stress; we all get pimples.

2. Hair products and oils need to be kept away from my face because this area is sensitive.
3. Electronic devices and hands remain away from my face. Change your pillowcase!
4. Stay calm because your PERIOD is coming #REDSLUSHIE

Don't forget! We are all uniquely created, so some girls are more prone to acne and pimples than others. Does that mean we tease or bully her? No! We use this time to uplift her with our words by saying something like, "We all get pimples at some point. It's ok." All girls go through hormonal changes. We all metamorphosize. Embrace the change!

You are altogether beautiful, my love; there is no flaw in you. Solomon 4:7

Jordan's Face Tips

Try to wash your face twice a day. Add this to your already created hygiene plan.

"Coconut oil and sugar scrub"
2 tsp. Of Coconut Oil
2 tsp. Of Sugar
2 slices of Cucumber

Directions: Combine all ingredients in a small bowl except for the cucumbers save those for your eyes. Stir the ingredients. Then, rub scrub in gentle circular motions for sixty seconds. Place sliced cucumbers over your eyes and relax. Once it dries, rinse with warm water.

"Honey Oatmeal Mask"
2 tsp of oatmeal (plain)
1 tsp of baking soda
1 tsp of honey

Directions: Mix together all ingredients in a small bowl. Slowly add water until it makes a paste like texture. Rub on your face in a circular motion. Sit back and relax for ten to fifteen

minutes. Rinse with warm water to close your pores.

Scrub or Mask? Ask your mom for help here. You can find other recipes that may work. Remember, everyone's skin is different. Seeing your face change can be embarrassing and scary. Just remember, puberty is nothing to be embarrassed about. God created you. Don't worry about what others think or say about you. What matters is what God says about you. God says you are beautiful, pimples and all!

Dear Diary,

Well, though I did not want to talk to her about what happened - my pimples or my feelings - praying with her always makes me calm. I just do not understand how my mom sees everything about me as beautiful. I have been praying that God will make me beautiful; but STILL, my prayers are not coming true. My mom told me I am wasting my prayers … that God already answered that prayer. She thinks she is a comedian.

I know I am pretty; I just don't feel like it with all this going on. I know feelings are real, and I have learned I am not to make decisions based on feelings. #FEELINGCHART

The feelings chart really helped me express my feelings. I will only admit it to you, but it really works. I am able to put words to my feelings.

During our talk, my mom made me rethink my life verse, and it is so true. My life verse is a scripture that my mom and dad prayed about for my life. It is a scripture that she wants me to live and claim over my life … and what are the odds that it fits me right now.

Charm is deceptive, and beauty is fleeting, but a woman who fears the Lord is to be praised. Proverbs 31:30

Memorizing your life verse is hard, but what makes it easier is understanding the meaning of the verse. This is like high school level learning we are doing here. Ok! Here is my break down of my life verse. READY?!

So, to me "charm is deceptive" means I cannot **solely** rely on my outer quality of pleasing others because it can be misleading to who God really calls me to be.

And, relying **solely** on my beauty is fleeting means outer beauty doesn't last a long time. What is so awesome about the next word "but" is that it is used to contrast the statement before it.

So, "but a woman," which is me, "who fears the lord" is to be praised. Now this phrase took me awhile to understand because I thought fear only meant "to be afraid of." But here "fears the Lord" means reverence Him. Even though I may be able to do everything - be charming and be beautiful - it means nothing if I do not acknowledge God as Lord of my life. Fear means knowing God is over everything and He is in charge of everything I do.

I have to keep that in my heart. I have to live in a way that honors God.

So yes, I am charming and beautiful; but most importantly, I fear the Lord.

#SO, SO, SO

So, how about you find a memory verse to claim over your life? Ask your mom for help? You may have one already. The bible may seem a little overwhelming at first. Just, start with a simple verse. When I entered first grade, I got my first real bible. My mom made a special day out of it. She got me this cool kit with highlighters and colorful tab things. I even got my name engraved on my bible. We took pictures. It was fun.

Jordan's Life Verse Tips: Memorize the scripture! Know what it means and how to apply it to your life. Break the scripture down to each individual word. Use the dictionary to find the meaning of each word. Last but not least; if you don't have or know any scripture, you can use mine! It is already written on your bookmark that came with this book! How awesome is that? We will have the same life verse, speak and claim it over your life now.

Pray for God to give you wisdom to understand the verse. After all, we are going through puberty and our brains can handle more complex and mature knowledge. Can't hurt praying for knowledge … can it?

Wisdom? So, this is a tough one to explain. Wisdom comes as we get older. For example, I was friends with a girl, and we had been friends since kindergarten. She started hanging with the popular group of girls and was not my friend anymore (well only when they were not around). She started picking on me ... like ... bullying me. It was horrible. But I wanted her to be my friend, so I just kept being friends with her. Guess what? There I sat one day in the office for bullying someone! Like ... are you kidding me?! And then came the call to my mom. She thought it was about my brother. I was in tears, freaking out. I had never been in the principal's office for anything bad in my entire life.

When I got home, my mom told me that birds of a feather flock together. I remember my snotty nose, saying, "But I did not do anything!" She told me it didn't matter, I was hanging with the wrong kinds of friends, and eventually I would become them. Of course, my mom is extra (she goes above and beyond); so, she freaked me out. She told me that if I am with a group of people in a car and they go to rob a bank, and I am in the car, I go to jail with the crew. Traumatizing mom, that's my mom (well, our mom). I was not going to jail. She told me I had to make wiser decisions.

I prayed to God for wisdom and started to just focus on my lessons, piano and cooking. My grades got back up to straight A's. The old group of girls made the principal's office their home. I was so glad I got wiser.

Also, Wisdom will come as we experience more things good and bad. The cool thing is wisdom can be taught. One lesson my mom taught me about wisdom was to be a wise steward of my resources. Yes, my mom was a girl scout leader and still teaches at vacation bible schools. I told you she is a super mom!

Resources are things you have. So, I try to keep my clothes neat, clean and organized. Who knows? I could pass those down to someone in need. My mom says when you give someone something make sure it is something you would use, and it is in good condition. So, I try my best!

She also taught me about being a good steward of my money. Money is a resource. She told me to always give to God first and to never spend all your money; saving is important. So, I try my best to be wise about my spending. I earn money from doing chores, and when my grandmother comes over she does pop up room checks, and I get paid just to keep my room clean. But you never know when she is coming, so I have to keep it clean. The main thing I keep cluttered is papers. I like to keep every paper I write on and draw on and every card someone gives me. I love greeting cards! It is so hard to throw away my paper. Overall, I try my best to be a good, wise steward of my resources.

Wisdom is more precious than rubies; nothing you desire can compare with her.
Proverbs 3:15

Jordan's Prayer Tips: If you have never prayed to God before, I want you to know it is pretty simple. My mom told me to talk with God like I would my friend because He is my friend. I don't have to worry about taking too much time out of God's busy day (because to me there are sick kids that need Him at St. Jude's), because God stands outside of time. He can be everywhere all at once. Can you say omnipresent? One time I was praying to God in my room, and I honestly thought I heard Him speaking to me. Then I realized it was my mom barging in my room, because you can't have locked doors in our house. Yep. Hard-knock life for me.

Chapter Four

Red Slushie

Dear Diary,

I know this chapter may gross some of you out. But it is actually very amazing to see how our bodies were created and how they work. It is a masterpiece. So, let's just jump right into this chapter. I know you are all thinking, "What is a red slushie?"

- *My favorite drink on a nice sunny day is a red slushie. I say red slushies. My mom says cherry slushies. Yes, I love slushies. As I was talking with my mom about my period, the slushie was all I kept thinking of. You know how when you go into the store and the slushie machine is not working properly and you get upset. Your slushie is just loose and kind of watery. Then when the machine is working there are clumps of ice in it. Well, that is kind of how I think about my period. At times your period, called menstruation, can produce a blood flow that is light or heavy. There can even be clots or clumps of* blood as well. Clots are just pieces of the uterus lining that haven't broken down all the way before they exit our vagina. My mom says this is completely normal. If you experience heavy bleeding continuously, don't panic; just alert your mom and plan a quick trip to your doctor.

Sounds disgusting … right? That is why I use the words **#REDSLUSHIE**.

All the girls at school use weird names like the rag, bloody mary, or your aunt flo is in town. Well, mine is red slushie.

Take a deep breath! Vagina? Clots? Blood? Uterus? Menstruation? What? Hopefully you have had a least part of the talk about your menstrual cycle with your mom by now. If not, it is ok. Better late than never.

Let me give you a visual that may help explain the fertility cycle. Moms do a good job at this, but visuals help too.

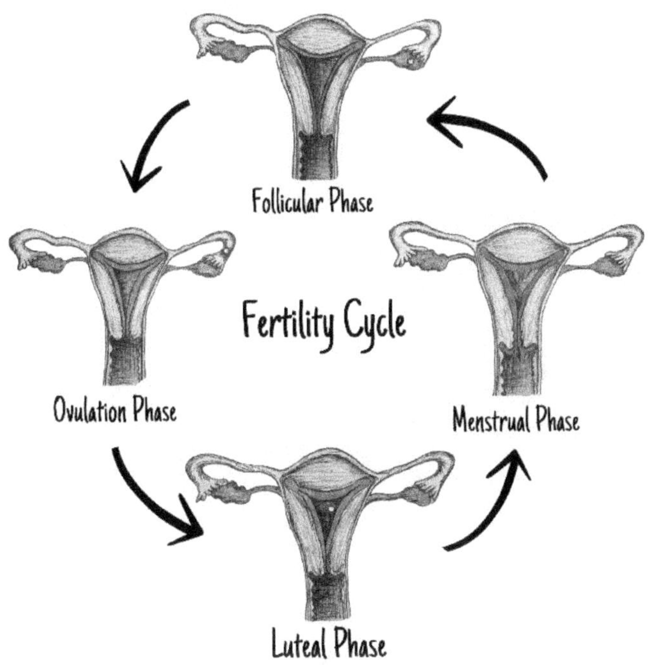

Follicular Phase
Fertility Cycle
Ovulation Phase
Menstrual Phase
Luteal Phase

Menstruation Phase

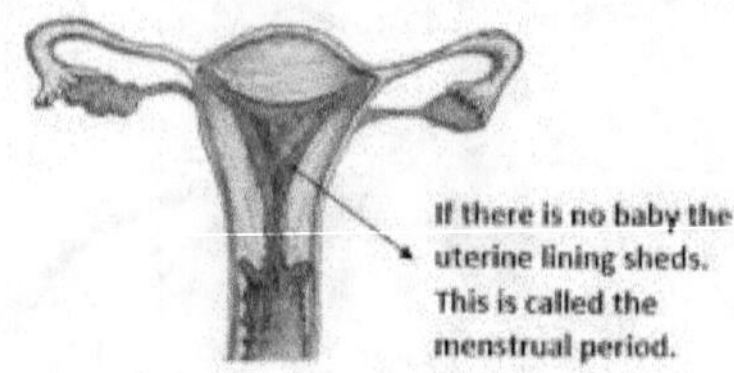

Follicular Phase

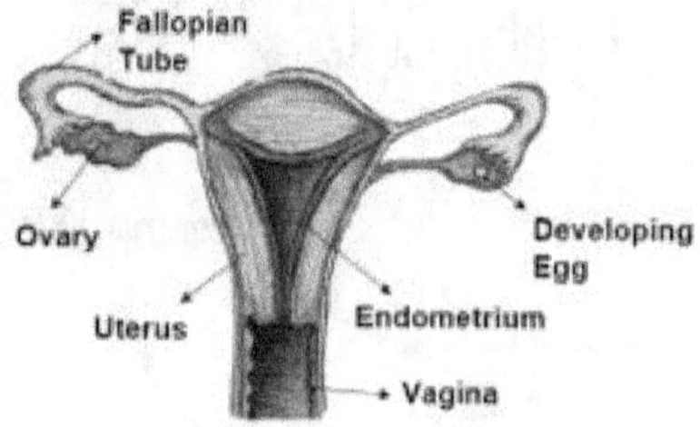

Ovulation Phase

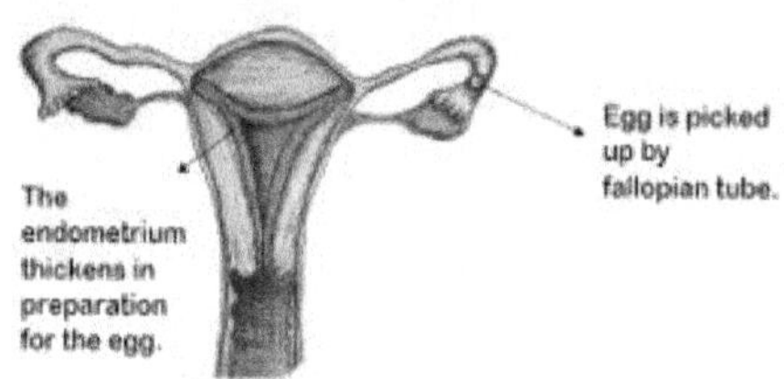

Luteal Phase

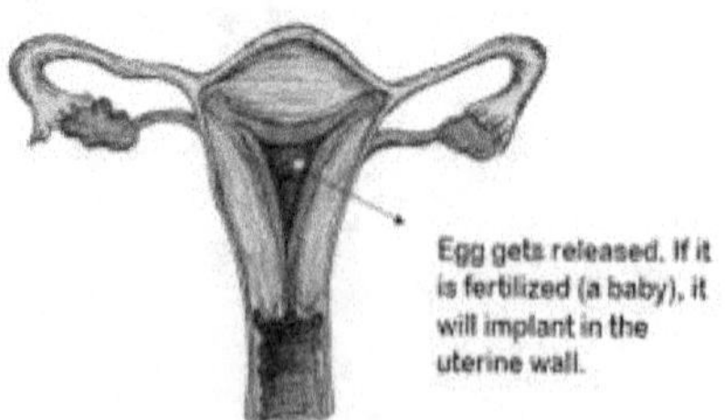

Now that I know more about my menstruation I feel more prepared for when it does happen. Last year, my mom started preparing me for the big talk. She had me create a survival kit just in case my period starts at school. My mom said her period started at school in fifth grade, so she is very persistent about preparing me. We went to the store, and I picked out a cute pencil pouch. Well, we did not put pencils in it. Instead we used it for a red slushie survival kit. It included an extra pair of panties, sanitary napkins (pads), a panty liner, wipes, and a sweet note from my mom.

Once the kit was complete, of course, my mom took the extra step of planning. If my period starts at school, I am to grab my survival kit and ask to go to the restroom.

If blood is present; then first, I breathe. She doesn't want me to overreact. If blood is just on the tissue I put on my panty liner or pad and proceed to the front office to call my mom.

Remember, your menstruation can start heavy or light. If blood is on my panties, I am to take them off and wrap in a paper towel and throw them in the trash. My mom says discarding them may not be the most sanitary way; but hey, desperate times. I grab my survival kit and attach the pad to my clean underwear. Then I tie my jacket around my waist and proceed to the front office. **#SHOPPINGDAYWITHMOM**

Yes, we have a survival plan and kit. Ask your mom to help! It's great mother/daughter bonding time.

Jordan's Tip: Waiting on your mom to arrive may take a while. That is why it is good to have more than one pad in your survival kit. Change or check your pad every two hours. At our school, the nurse is located in the front office and has extra pads if you need some.

Warning: Wear darker colored uniform bottoms. Everyone at school does not need to know you have had your period. Carry a jacket with you every day to school in case there is some spotting on your uniform.

So, of course, my mom is extra. She made me act the scene out. So, we pretended that my cycle started at school; and she walked me through the scenario four times. I was having information overload. That night I dreamed I got my period and forgot what to do.

This was not the first time my mom did this acting out stuff. One time when I was five, she talked to me about stranger danger. Well, let's just say she taught me self-defense at five! Who does that? Her! She taught it at my school. She pretended to try to kidnap me with candy, ice cream, puppies … you get the point. Well, she picked me up and tried to take me. I had to physically kick, punch, and scream ... yes! … at this crazy lady who is my mom. For a moment I forgot she was my mom. This was in front of my entire class. YES! Then she did it with other kids, and they raised

their hands to be chosen to participate.
Can you say traumatizing? #CRAYCRAY

Dear Diary,

*   After thinking and laughing at my mom and how crazy she is, I realized how valuable everything is that she has taught and demonstrated to me. She had a talk with me when I turned eight and told me her story. Evil things happened to my mom when she turned eight. People touched her breast buds and vagina. My mom was abused and mistreated. She told me that sometimes evil things happen to good people. She has taught me not to be naive … evil people do exist. Her story made me feel sad, angry, and I must admit, a little afraid. However; she reassured me that no matter what happens to me - good or bad - she is my safe person. I can go to her with anything no matter how bad I think it is. I know for sure my mom loves me and that God loves me more.*

How precious is your unfailing love, O God! Psalm 36:7

PMS (Premenstrual Syndrome)

Usually, before your period comes, your body may give you signs a few days before that signal your menstrual cycle is about to start. I have made a short list of PMS signs that my mom shared with me. I am sure there are more. I put a check by the ones I have had.

- ✓ Mood Changes
- ✓ Pimples
- ✓ Sore breast
- ✓ Food cravings
    (I usually don't eat a lot, but I have been hungry. My mom told me just to be more active and make healthy choices ... not to solely focus on diets. I am a kid.)
- ✓ **HEADACHES**
- ✓ Stomach Cramps

(My mom says warm compresses and
hot tea helps for this. Hot tea ... very
fancy)

As you can see, I bolded headaches;
and later I will tell you why.

When you first get your cycle,
recognizing your PMS symptoms will help
you keep track of when your cycle is
coming so you can be more prepared. Yes,
this will happen normally once a month. At
the beginning it can be irregular, meaning
not the same. It is normal in the beginning
if your period doesn't come the next month
or start on the exact date. Your body will
eventually regulate and will be like
clockwork ... right on time.

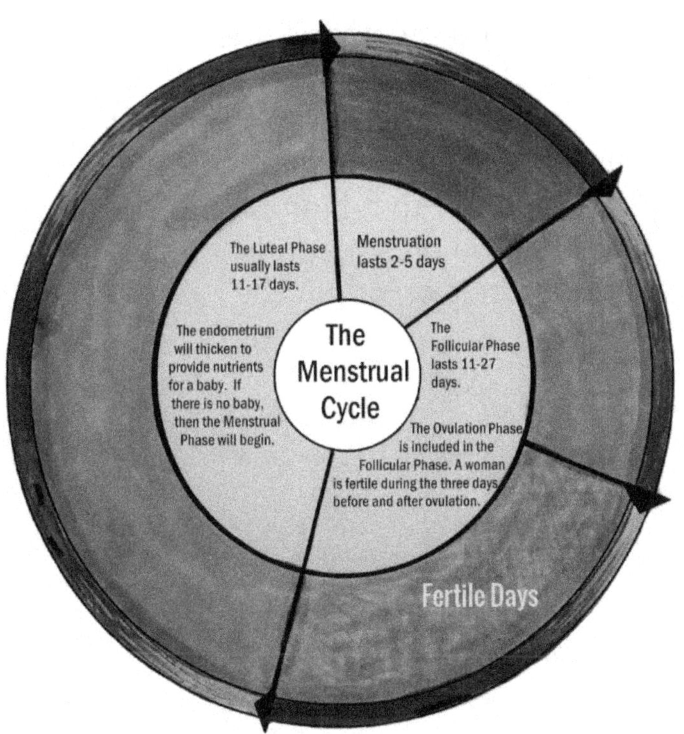

I have created a HelloFlo calendar. HelloFlo will help you calculate when your cycle is due so you can be prepared and have your survival kit on hand. We made a sample one to teach me how to calculate my menstrual cycle, and I haven't even got my period yet. #REDSLUSHIE

If you have already started your cycle, my mom suggests that you give the charting about three months and see if you see some patterns. By six months we all should be regular. From then on out you will know what the girls mean when the say my aunt Flo is in town.

Jordan's HelloFlo Calendar
#RedSlushie

Sunday	Monday	Tuesday	Wednesday	Thursday	Friday	Saturday
1 **PMS** Pimples	2 **PMS** Sore buds	3 **PMS** Migraines	4 **REDSLUSHIE** **DAY 1** heavy flow	5 Cramps DAY 2 heavy	6 Moody DAY 3 normal	7 Be Active DAY 4 normal
8 DAY 5 light	9 **BYE FLO** DAY 6	10 **FREE** DAY 7	11 DAY 8	12 DAY 9	13 DAY 10	14 DAY 11
15 DAY 12	16 DAY 13	17 DAY 14	18 DAY 15	19 DAY 16	20 DAY 17	21 DAY 18
22 DAY 19	23 DAY 20	24 DAY 21	25 DAY 22	26 DAY 23	27 DAY 24	28 DAY 25
29 **PMS** DAY 26	30 **PMS** DAY 27	31 **PMS** DAY 28	1 **REDSLUSHIE** Aunt Flo in town **DAY 1**	2	3	4
5	6	7	8	9	10	11

Jordan's Tips: Bathing is very important during your cycle. There is a Hello Flo app that can be helpful for keeping track of your menstrual cycle.

Make sure to check in with your doctor and go to regular checkups. Your body is going through a lot of changes physically, mentally and emotionally.

Migraines (Headaches)

I am scared to write about this part, but my mom has taught me to be fearless. It is hard sometimes; but I will be really vulnerable.

I am scared to have my period, because I do not like to see blood. The main reason is that one of the side effects could be increased headaches.

(I'm thinking about my dream of working at St. Jude's hospital and finding cures for cancer and other rare disease; so, I must be able to handle the sight of blood ... right??? But, right now my feelings about blood coming out of my vagina is very disgusting.)

Have you ever had a headache before?

At the age of four I began having headaches. Then when I was five, I was diagnosed with severe migraines with seizure like activity. I had to go to so many doctors and have so many tests run on me. I was in pain and very afraid.

I know God says fear not. But when I have a migraine, it feels like a hammer is drilling in my head and I am about to die. It is hard to open my eyes; everything is very blurry. I go into a deep sleep, and when I awake, I do not remember anything. I have to take all these preventive medicines and have them at school with me. I have not had a migraine in a very long time and that is why I am so scared.

I know I am not to fear death, but I do not want to die! My mom helped me memorize a scripture: Even though I walk through the darkest valley, I will fear no evil, for your rod and staff comfort me. Psalm 23:4

That means that God is with me even in the deepest valley, when I am most afraid. So, I do not have to fear because He is with me.

My mom wrote me a letter when I was in the hospital.

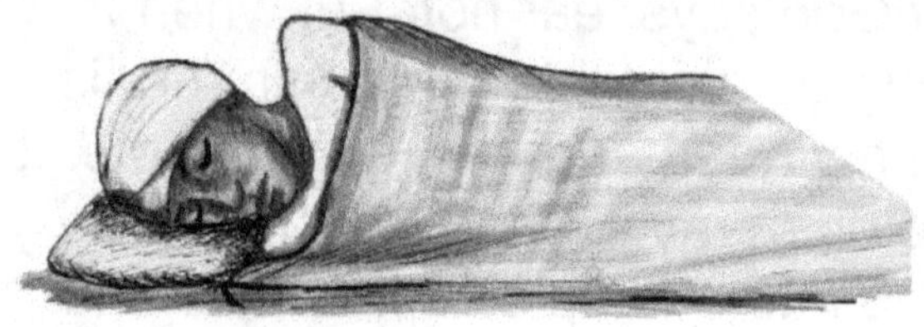

My sweetest Jordan,

From the moment you were born I knew you were special. I held your two-pound body in my hands. The staff thought you were not going to make it, and you did. I know you are afraid and, at times, very sad. If I could take all the pain away, I would. Oh, my sweet child, I want you to know I love you more than anything. But God loves you more. He loved you when you were being formed in my womb. He loved you so much, He gave His son Jesus to die for you. And because of that you have a place called Heaven to go to. I know you fear dying, but I want you to know there is no death for those in Christ. So, do not be afraid, God is with you and the Holy Spirit lives in you.

Love, Your Mom.

When I was 8, I was baptized and, honestly, it helped me overcome my fear of death if that makes sense. My mom says all kids go to heaven. I believe so, too.

Baptism is when you accept God and Jesus into your heart. It is just a symbol of my love and decision to follow Christ. When you know right from wrong and understand sin, you may be ready to get baptized.

My baptism was pretty cool. I was a little nervous about all the people seeing me; but I knew it was my time. My family and church family gathered in the back room and created a huge circle, and they prayed over me. I signed my name on the wall of my church. I walked into a big hot tub. Before I went under the water, my pastor asked me a question. He said, "Jordan, do you accept Jesus as your Lord and Savior?" I immediately thought about Jesus on the cross and how he will be with me forever, and I said a huge YES. He said, "I baptize you, my sister, in the name of the Father, the Son and the Holy Spirit;" and there I was soaking wet and baptized. I love you God!

That is my baptism story. Do you have one?

Jordan Tips: Baptism is an outward public symbol of an inward decision to follow Christ. It usually comes after you have prayed the prayer of salvation. Talk with your mom about your salvation. Best decision I ever made! #SALVATIONSEALED

Simple Prayer of Salvation

Dear God,

I know that I am a sinner; and I need You and Your forgiveness. I believe in your son Jesus and what He did for me by dying on the cross. I accept Him as my Lord and Savior. I want to follow Jesus the rest of my life. Amen.

The Big Question

Dear Diary,

Ok God, here is my big question, "Why do women have periods?" Also, why did I ask my mom, too?

My mom tells loooong stories. Did I tell you she was a storyteller at church? Yes, she is like a super woman or something. But she is a pretty good storyteller. She used to read to my oldest brother, and I like every night, and then she stopped. We had to read on our own. Then, when my baby brother arrived, she started reading to him. So, now we get to sit and listen to her read to him. I still like when she reads to me! Below is my mom's big story when I asked her. Here she goes.

Dear Jordan,

I am so glad you asked that question.

When God created man, man was on a perfect Earth. Man did not have to work. Man enjoyed a perfect place in relationship with God. Man had access to all the food *he wanted. Then, God created a garden a special garden (God is the first master gardener) for man to oversee. Then He told man, "You can eat anything you want, but not from one tree. The tree of knowledge of good and evil." God told man if he ate from that tree he would die.*

Then, after God said everything was good, He had a thought. Nope, He thought, everything is not quite as good as I would like it. He realized it is not good for man to be alone. Always remember humans need relationships.

On the same day, God said, "I will make him a helper suitable for him."

God continued from creating man and created for man a woman in one day.

"God created man in his own image and the image of God he created male and female He created them." Genesis 1:27

He told them to be fruitful and multiply. He told them to fill the Earth.

In order for you to be fruitful, your body must have a menstrual cycle. You, my dear were uniquely created to give and carry life. A man cannot have a menstrual cycle. A man does not have a uterus. A man does not have ovaries. A man was not designed to carry and deliver a life, only a woman.

This is why there is no shame in getting your period; it is actually a celebration. It is a sign that your body is properly functioning the way it is designed to function. I had a hard time carrying life. I want you to understand that having a normal cycle, carrying and giving life is a blessing. There is no shame in it.

"When God saw all that He had created He said, 'It is VERY good.'" Genesis 1:31

In the beginning you asked me if God was part woman. My dear, God is not part of anything. God is everything, complete and perfect. Humans are designed to reflect Him.

Remember, "The earth is the Lord's and everything in it, the world and all who live in it." Psalm 24:1

Dear Diary,

After having that talk with my mom, I feel so special. No man can have a baby. God put Adam into a deep sleep just to create woman.

When I think about the fact that God made me and my body for a purpose it makes me proud of being a woman (though I am not a full woman yet, but a female). Having a menstrual cycle is a special gift that I was given in order to be able to carry life. I do not have to be ashamed of my body, my skin, my hair or my teeth. I am who I am, and I am pretty cute.

I have learned that I do not have to fear changes and the 'what ifs. I just need to trust God and know God is with me.

One day, I will be a great mom. I am going to be caring and loving. I am going to talk with my daughter about her body so she will know how special she is, just like my mom did with me. I will tell her she is fearfully and wonderfully made.

I am beautiful just as I am. I am beautiful because the God who created me is beautiful, and He lives in me. I am perfectly created, because God says I am. I am valuable, because Jesus died for me. He paid the cost for me. I am chosen! I am loved!

My mom says I am a treasure. She told me that my body and my soul is a rare, valuable treasure. I do not have to be out there hunting for a boyfriend or a husband ... that God has the man for me, and he will find me in God's timing. Until then, I just focus on my relationship with God and reverence Him.

My older brother loves dinosaurs and sharks. My mom bought him an expensive dinosaur dig kit for Christmas. It took my brother three months of digging and brushing to find a fossil of a t-rex. When he found the fossil, he was so happy he put that fossil on his dresser and takes really good care of it. My mom said he values it more because he had to work hard and long to get it. He treasures that fossil. Every time he talks about the t-rex he mentions that dig kit and how long it took him to find it.

She said that treasure is just like me, so I do not have to rush the finding process. It will come! I am a rare TREASURE, and so are you!

But you are a chosen people, His royal priesthood, a holy nation, God's special treasure, that you may shine forth His goodness and grace to others, because He called you out the dark world into the light of His kingdom. 1 Peter 2:9

Chapter Five

K·I·S·S·I·N·G·S

Dear Diary,

The girls at school can be very messy. They want to tell everyone's business, like a gossip girl group. They tell everyone who is on their periods.

When I was walking down the fifth-grade hallway, I heard some fifth-grade girls talking about mature stuff like boyfriends. One girl said she had kissed a boy and they were talking about it.

Every day one of my friends keeps asking me who do I have a crush on. She said, "Jordan, you have to like someone." I didn't answer. If I did answer her she was going to sing that stupid song. Jordan and somebody sitting in a tree K I S S I N G. First comes love, then marriage ... blah, blah. The song is just not funny to me.

She passed me a note in class telling me who likes me and that I have to like someone. I wrote her back, telling her, if I did, I would not tell her. She said, "Come on, Jordan!" So, I drew her a picture of who I like, and I said, "This is who I like."

I sent her a picture of the loading sign. Classic. I laughed so hard. I wrote underneath, "Girl, Bye! I don't have to like anybody, and I am not kissing anybody."

Well, she didn't send the note back. Oh well.

At recess I sat under a tree with my journal, and I was thinking, what is a kiss anyway? Honestly, I think kissing a boy at our age is inappropriate. I am sounding just like my mom. My mom told me to always try to see things the way God sees it. Sometimes it is hard to see; but with this one it is easy. Hello, bacteria!

To me, a kiss is a symbol of love. It is valuable and special. Right mom? I just thought about that picture on the side of their bed. When she and my dad met they were kissing. I will ask her when I get

*home. My mom was K I S S I N G. She will
have to explain herself. Yep!*
  Mission: interrogate mom

Jordan Fun Facts: In some cultures,
kissing is a sign of greeting. But that is not
the type of "KISSING" my friend was
talking about. My mom and dad told me I
am not to kiss anyone ... period ... on the
lips, not even family.

... ₒoO**O**

"Hey mom"

"Hey. How was school?"

"Well, it was okay; but I have some
questions for you before I take a bath."

"Okay. If it is about shaving again, the
answer didn't change."

"It is not about shaving. So, you know I
was trying to be honest about my feelings. I
am confused. In the last few weeks we

have been doing some serious bonding, and you have told me everything. But I thought about it at school. You met dad when you were sixteen. **SO**, yall were already kissing? You are telling me not to kiss anybody; but you were kissing daddy at the age of sixteen. A kiss is valuable!!!!! You gave up your lips. I am just asking an honest question from what I have observed. I finally caught you off guard. You have no answer."

"Well, Jordan, I must say more is caught than taught. I didn't have this talk when I was your age. I didn't understand how valuable I was. So, I made choices that were outside the will of God for my life. I was living a sinful life. So yes, your dad and I did kiss and make decisions that were not in line with the way God desired them to be. I will never forget the day God told me the way I was living was wrong. I had been dating your father for nine years. Three of those years we had been living together. I talked with my grandfather and he said why should your dad buy the cow

when the milk is free? It finally clicked. I
was doing and playing the role as wife; but
I was not. I went to talk with your dad.
Nervously, I told him I can no longer live
this way. You can either marry me or we
will separate. We were married one year
later. As I grew closer to God, I began to
see and value myself. Then you were born
and, immediately, I realized how important
it is for me to equip you with the talk I never
had. No one is perfect. Mistakes will
happen. However; because we serve a
good, good Father He gives us grace,
mercy and forgiveness for our wrongs.
Once I repented, God erased my wrongs.
Gone. Blotted out. So, my dear, I am your
super mom and I am on top of my game,
chick! I was waiting on that question, and I
have written the ending of that poem."

I was a broken girl
From nowhere
I never had this talk before,
Like I said.

But even if I did,

Jesus does forgive.
But now that I am found,
With this talk
I can turn all around.

Shine, shine, bright girl
Soar away.

I have equipped you
With all you need.
I have done my part
I have planted His seed.

Shine, shine, bright girl
Soar away.

Jesus Christ is home
for girls like me;
And in He,
Captives are set free!

Embrace the Change!!!

Dear Jordan,

I am He who created you. I know every hair on your head and body. Do not be afraid of the world. I have overcome the world. Do not be afraid of the "what ifs" you keep thinking about. Yes, I know your thoughts. Some of your questions, your brain will never fully understand. I want you to know that it is ok not to know everything about me. I want you to trust what you do know about me. I will never leave you. You are my child. The day you were baptized I was there. I saw you and I filled you with my Holy Spirit. I live in you, so I am always with you. Even if you mess up, remember Jordan, your mess is never to messy for me to clean up. No one will ever be perfect. My love for you is free and unconditional. I love everything about you, my darling.

You are brave and courageous.

You are safe and protected.

You are beautiful and flawless.

You are loved by me.

My arms will forever embrace you. **NOW** *you embrace the change!*

Shine, shine, bright girl! Soar away!

Love, Your God!

Isaiah 60:1 ... ***Arise, shine, for your light has come, and the glory of the LORD rises upon you.***

JUST FOR MOMS

Dear Moms,

My name is Shermane. I am so grateful that you have taken the time to purchase and go through this book with your daughter. I always believe it is very important that we know a little about the author(s) and what the author(s) of a Christian book believes in before we expose our children to their beliefs through their writings. So, I want to take some time to tell you what I believe in, a little of my story, and give you some advice for starting healthy conversations with your daughter.

What do I believe? I am a grateful believer and follower of Jesus Christ. I believe in the Holy Trinity which is God the Father, God the Son and the Holy Spirit. I believe they are co-equal parts of one God.

I believe Jesus is the son of God. He was born of a virgin birth. He died for our sins and rose from the grave with all power. He ascended to Heaven and will return as King of Kings.

I believe the bible is God's Word written by humans under the guidance of the Holy Spirit which lives in us from the moment of salvation. I believe that God is the Creator of all things. I believe man is made in the image of God and sin separates us from God. I believe eternal life begins the moment we receive Jesus Christ into our lives by faith.

So, what's my story? I was born in Alexandria, Louisiana. My mom was a single mom of two kids. When I was three months old, my mom married my stepfather and my younger brother was conceived. I have never had a relationship with my biological father. He was incarcerated for ten years and once released he continued his life without knowing me or my older brother.

I was raised from birth in church. I came from a family of pastors, preachers, deacons and religious leaders. As a child, I always knew of God. My mother faithfully took us to church and not just on Sundays. We basically lived there.

However, behind closed doors my home was abusive. My mom and I never had a very intimate mother daughter relationship. She did provide the physical things a child needs, but she was never present verbally, emotionally or mentally for the maternal needs.

My mom never had the talk about life or being a young lady with me. When my cycle began, she did talk to me, but it was too late because I had already been abused. She was physically abused in our home; and at the early age of 8 I was abused in all ways.

It continued for years. My mom stayed in an abusive marriage for 26 years. But one thing she did believe was teaching us about God. We always went to Sunday school, choir rehearsal, bible study and, of course, Sunday church service as the perfect family.

"Start children off on the way they should go, and even when they are old they will not turn from it." Proverbs 22:6

I always was an honor roll student, and I loved to read. I hid everything that went on in my home from all my friends. But on the inside, I was withdrawn, overweight and struggled with self-love.

Around the age of 12, I did consider suicide. I had begun to dislike God, and I believed that He was not who I thought He was. I had believed in a loving God, and to me He was not.

I got my first job at 15. I met my husband at 15. I graduated high school early. I left home for college in Monroe, Louisiana and never returned home. I would call and check on my mom maybe twice a month.

I worked from the age of 15 and all through college full time. I went to church occasionally. Then one day in college, I saw I could take religion class as an elective. I thought that is an easy A because I knew all I needed to know about Him.

It was such an easy A, I decided I would take another religion class and I did. I started having flashbacks of abuse and God; and I passed the course, but I never took another religion class. I ended up in an on- campus counseling group.

Well, the beginning of my junior year, I moved off campus into an apartment and my boyfriend, now husband, moved with me. Then came more bills. So, I needed to get another job. I did and went to college part-time. I got a better paying job and college slowly faded away. This job eventually led me to Lafayette, La. My boyfriend, now husband, moved with me as well.

At the age of 24, we were married. One year later, I conceived a girl, Ivy. However, at six months pregnant, Ivy was delivered deceased. Five months later, I conceived again, a girl, Miracle. I prayed and fasted so hard, even asked God to forgive me, and at six and a half months, Miracle was delivered deceased. I was so disappointed in God. I did not conceive again for two years.

Then in 2008, I conceived again, a girl. At 24 weeks pregnant my sac began leaking; and I was admitted into the hospital where I remained on bedrest for 7 weeks. Other than my husband, I had no family in town. I stared at the gray walls and began talking to God. At 31 weeks, I awoke and told my nurse that my daughter will arrive today and to call the doctor.

My mom and husband were present, as the NICU unit prepared all the machines in the operating room. Jordan was born at 31 weeks. My mom said, "Jordan had a glow around her." Jordan weighed 2 pounds and

15 ounces. She was never on a breathing machine; she was breathing on her own. Even the staff was shocked. She stayed in the NICU unit for only 4 weeks.

The moment I held her I knew two things and I feared one thing. I would teach her about God. I would not let anyone abuse her. I feared that someone would abuse her.

The "Talk"

I began having this talk when Jordan was one year old. I would read her books about God. I knew I was supposed to teach her about God. I did learn that from my mom.

I was so protective of Jordan. She was never left alone with anyone. When she was 2 years old, I started teaching Jordan about her body parts. I never used street names or nicknames for her body parts.

When she turned 3, I decided to put her in a mother's day out program for two days a week. The summer before Jordan started, I talked with her about healthy and unhealthy touch. I started having mild panic attacks in the middle of the conversation. She was enrolled in the program and that gave me some free time. My husband and I finally found a church home, so I signed up for a bible study.

I continued to pour into Jordan. But for some reason I struggled with that loving Father part. I still had self-love issues. God spoke to me and said, "How are you going to tell her how much God loves her when you don't think I love you?" Also, I will never forget the words of my pastor saying more is caught than taught.

I had taught my daughter the knowledge of God; but it was nothing if I did not model it for her. So, I surrendered all my hurts, anger and distrust over to God. I realized I had generations of abuse and silence in my family. I feared it would repeat itself with my daughter. So, I began my journey of healing, transforming, and developing an intimate relationship with God.

The talk about God began to come so naturally. As she got older I realized it was more than the talk. I had broken a generational curse. I felt chains falling.

"He brought them out of darkness, and the shadow of death. And broke away their chains" Psalm 107:14

"So now, I will break his yoke bar from upon you. And I will tear off your shackles." Nahum 1:13

I know I cannot protect her from everything that may come her way, but I have equipped her with all she needs. I trust God will handle everything and the Holy Spirit will guide her throughout her life. I am merely a steward watching over God's possession. She does not belong to me. God has entrusted me with a very precious, unique, and valuable resource, His child. He has entrusted you as well.

Maintaining Healthy Conversations

Remember moms that your daughter is not only going through physical changes, but also psychological and emotional changes. Make puberty exciting! Make sure you pay attention to her and actively listen to her needs.

Privacy and personal space will become very important to her. Jordan can now lock her door if she is changing, and we all have to knock first before entering.

This is also a time when your daughter may start to find her own identity. Reassure your daughter of her beauty with words of affirmation. With social media, television, and magazines finding her identity may be challenging. This may cause additional anxiety, and in some teens, depression. Please do not hesitate to seek help from her doctor.

Allow your daughter some independence and responsibility. Let her lead in some activities. She will be creating decision making skills and understanding consequences, which are a necessity in this life. Spend quality time with your daughter; but always remember you are the parent and she is your daughter. My daughter is not my confidante.

Finally, my most important piece of advice ... if you have problems with loving yourself, I strongly advise you to work on yourself. Always remember more is caught than taught. This means no matter how much we teach them with words, their eyes are fixed on our walk. We are their walking example. We are to reflect the walking example we were given. Jesus Christ is our example.

"To this you were called, because Christ suffered for you, leaving you an example, that you should follow his steps."
1 Peter 2: 21

Spark the Talk Activity Pages

My mom and I pray that you and your mom would spend time doing these short activities together. Feel free to go back through the book to look for answers.

Define

Draw a line to match the word with the proper definition.

1. Metamorphosis
2. Catastrophe

3. Baptism
4. Salvation
5. Self-conscious

6. Reverence

7. Omnipresent

a. Everywhere all at once
b. Deep respect and honor
c. Transformation
d. Aware of oneself
e. Saving from sin (wrong) which comes from Jesus, needing His help to save
f. Event causing suffering (pimples, period)
g. Outward symbol of an inward decision to follow Jesus

Those were some big words. On this journey with God, you will hear these words used a lot. Well, maybe not the word metamorphosis!

Word Search

Can you find the hidden words? Circle the words you find. Happy Searching!

Find: Metamorphosis; Catastrophe; PMS; Baptism; Salvation; Reverence; Hygiene; Vagina, Uterus, Bud.

The Journey

L C H N K M W C E I O C
O O U O I E T V G U R O
C A T A S T R O P H E F
C Z E B V A G I N A V S
Y M R J G M O D Z C E A
H X U P O O O C O J R L
J B S E K R L N Y D E V
X U F B A P T I S M N A
D D X D S H M P F A C T
C D F X X S S S O S E I
I U H Y G I E N E B J O
Y Z Y P T S P A U P I N

Female Reproductive System

Label the body parts below with their proper anatomical names.

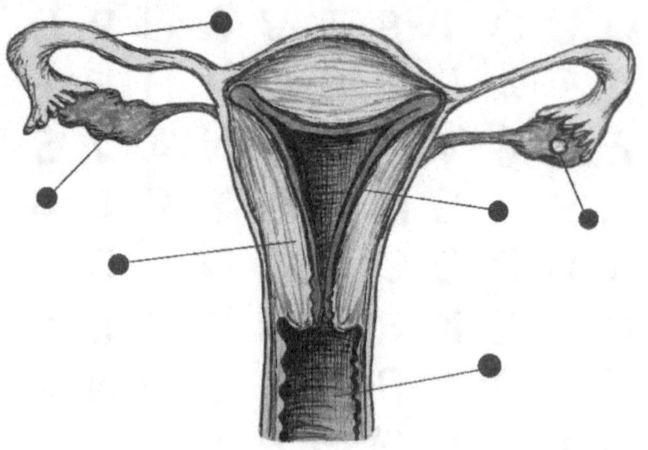

Decision Making

There will be no answer key for this portion. My mom and I have prayed that this portion would spark healthy conversations.

Moms, please give the girls time to answer the questions on their own then proceed to having some healthy conversations. Take time to read the Just for Moms section. Finally, please respect your daughters' honesty.

Girls answer the questions below.

If your mom had not given you the talk, and you were to start your period now, would you tell your mom? Do you feel prepared to talk about your body with your mom?

If the gossip group of girls were calling your friend "period girl" and telling everyone that she got her period, and you were with her, what would you do? What does God think about gossiping?

If your friends all had boyfriends and were pressuring you to get a boyfriend, what would you do?

Do you think you are beautiful? What do you honestly think about your body?

How do you feel when you talk about your body parts and menstruation?

Do you have a safe adult in your life? Who is that person to you?

How do you feel when you think about God uniquely creating you?

What do you think about salvation and baptism?

Answer Key: Definitions 1.c 2. f 3. g 4. e 5. d 6. b 7.a

We would love to hear about your conversations and experiences with our book. Email us at
JCREEDshines@gmail.com